# first
# animal
## encyclopedia
## rainforests

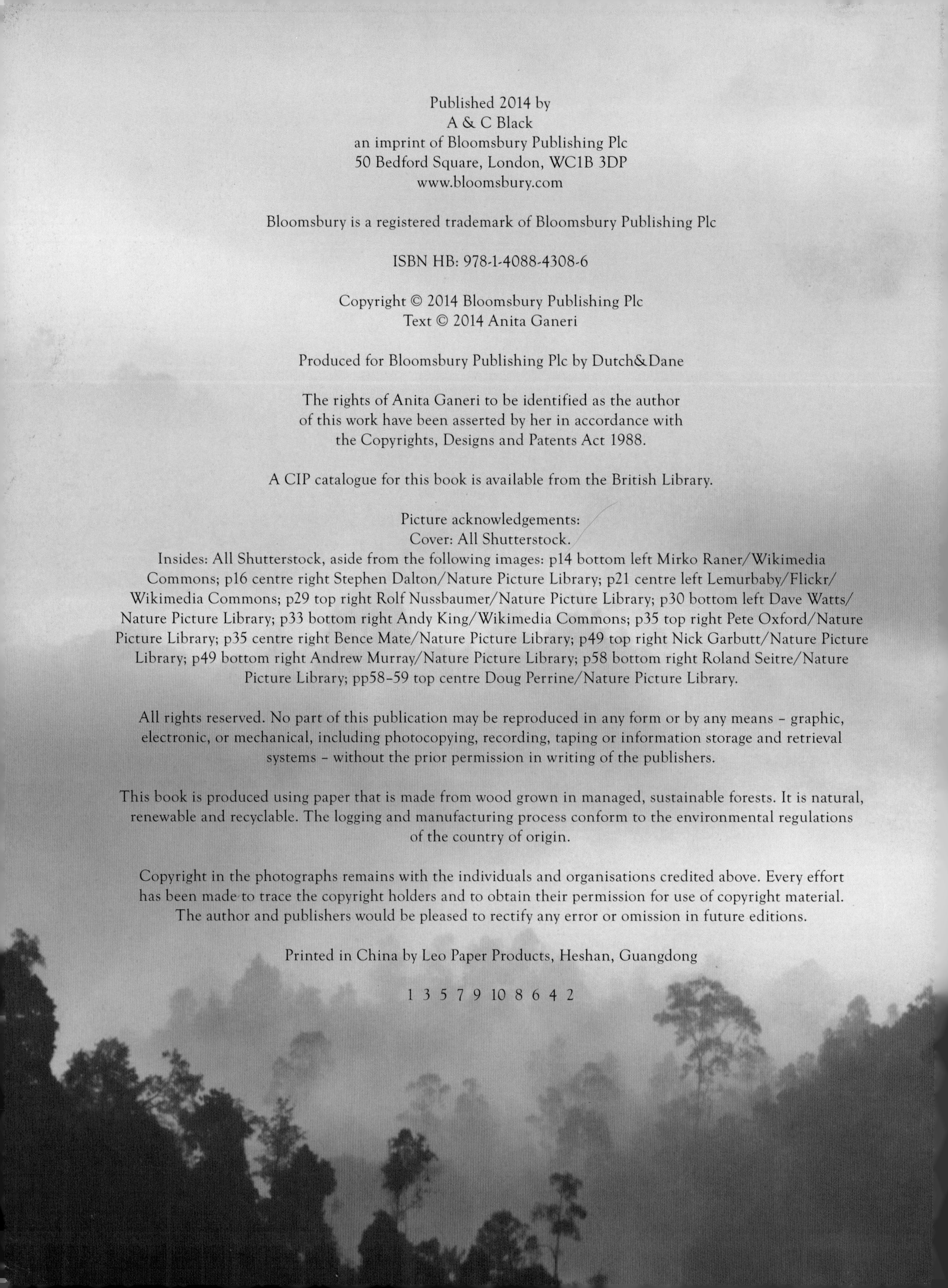

Published 2014 by
A & C Black
an imprint of Bloomsbury Publishing Plc
50 Bedford Square, London, WC1B 3DP
www.bloomsbury.com

Bloomsbury is a registered trademark of Bloomsbury Publishing Plc

ISBN HB: 978-1-4088-4308-6

Copyright © 2014 Bloomsbury Publishing Plc
Text © 2014 Anita Ganeri

Produced for Bloomsbury Publishing Plc by Dutch&Dane

The rights of Anita Ganeri to be identified as the author
of this work have been asserted by her in accordance with
the Copyrights, Designs and Patents Act 1988.

A CIP catalogue for this book is available from the British Library.

Picture acknowledgements:
Cover: All Shutterstock.
Insides: All Shutterstock, aside from the following images: p14 bottom left Mirko Raner/Wikimedia
Commons; p16 centre right Stephen Dalton/Nature Picture Library; p21 centre left Lemurbaby/Flickr/
Wikimedia Commons; p29 top right Rolf Nussbaumer/Nature Picture Library; p30 bottom left Dave Watts/
Nature Picture Library; p33 bottom right Andy King/Wikimedia Commons; p35 top right Pete Oxford/Nature
Picture Library; p35 centre right Bence Mate/Nature Picture Library; p49 top right Nick Garbutt/Nature Picture
Library; p49 bottom right Andrew Murray/Nature Picture Library; p58 bottom right Roland Seitre/Nature
Picture Library; pp58–59 top centre Doug Perrine/Nature Picture Library.

This book is produced using paper that is made from wood grown in managed, sustainable forests. It is natural,
renewable and recyclable. The logging and manufacturing process conform to the environmental regulations
of the country of origin.

Printed in China by Leo Paper Products, Heshan, Guangdong

1 3 5 7 9 10 8 6 4 2

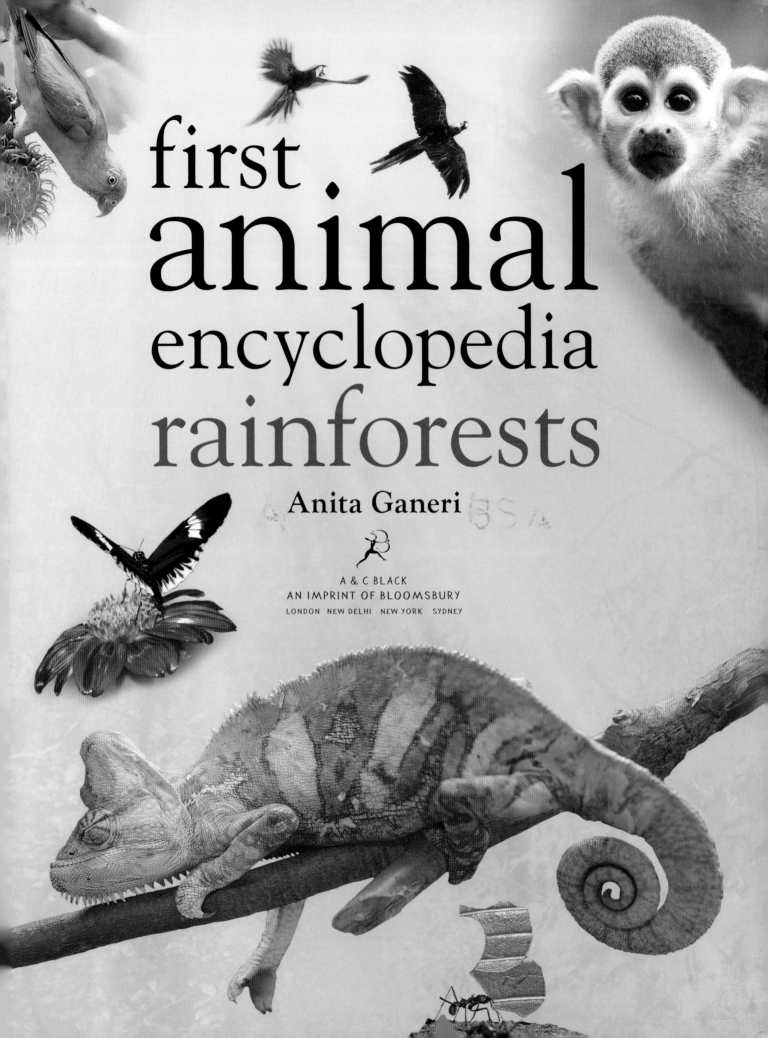

# first
# animal
# encyclopedia
# rainforests

### Anita Ganeri

A & C BLACK
AN IMPRINT OF BLOOMSBURY
LONDON   NEW DELHI   NEW YORK   SYDNEY

# Contents

# Rainforest life

Tropical rainforests grow along the equator, where it is hot, rainy and steamy all year round. They are home to millions of animals – more than anywhere else on Earth. Animals can find lots of food here, as well as many hiding places.

North America
Europe
Asia
Southeast Asia
India
The Philippines
Equator
Africa
Brazil
Sumatra
Borneo
New Guinea
South America
Madagascar
Australia

◀ The tropical parts of the world are found to the north and south of the equator.

▲ The rainforests are shown in green.

## Blooming forests
Rainforests grow mainly in India and Southeast Asia, West and Central Africa, and South America. There are also patches along the northeast coast of Australia and in New Guinea. The biggest rainforest grows along the banks of the River Amazon in Brazil.

## Warm and wet
It always feels warm and sticky in the rainforest, with temperatures reaching around 25°C in the day and at night. It rains almost every day – at least 2,000 millimetres of rain falling every year.

Rainforests cover only about a sixth of the Earth's surface. But they are home to half of all the world's known species of animals, more than any other habitat.

▲ A baby orangutan learns how to swing through the trees.

## Forest layers

Rainforest trees grow in layers, depending on how tall they are. The tallest are the emergents, which tower above everything. Below them is the canopy. Underneath is the understorey – and then, finally, the dark and gloomy forest floor. Each layer has its own particular types of plants and animals.

◄ Toucans are famous for their brightly coloured beaks.

▶ Ants are the most common rainforest animals. These leaf-cutter ants are collecting materials to take back to their nest.

# High in the treetops

Towering throughout the rainforest is a scattering of giant trees, called emergents. They can grow to more than 60 metres tall – that's as high as a 20-storey building! Even though they are often battered by howling winds, they are still home to many different types of animals.

## Swooping eagles

A harpy eagle from South America perches on a branch, on the lookout for food. When it spots a sloth or a howler monkey, it swoops down at high speed and grabs its prey with its huge talons (claws).

▲ Emergent trees stretch upwards, many metres into the air.

► Harpy eagles build their nests high up in the trees.

▶ A colugo resting on a tree trunk, with its 'wings' folded away.

## Super gliders

Colugos live in the rainforests of Southeast Asia, where they glide among the emergent trees. They are the size of squirrels and their legs are joined by folds of furry skin. They stretch out their legs to use these folds as wings.

◀ This agile spider monkey is hanging by its tail.

## Spider monkeys

These monkeys spend their lives in the treetops of South America, searching for fruit to eat. They get their name from their long, spindly, spider-like arms and legs. Expert climbers, they use their long tails to grab on to branches and swing from one to another.

## AWESOME!

The tallest trees in the rainforest are tualang trees. They grow in Southeast Asia and can reach a dizzy 90 metres in height! There are no branches growing on these trees until about halfway up their trunks.

# Under the canopy

The canopy stretches out beneath the emergent trees like a thick, green roof of leaves. It bursts with life and colour, and is home to two-thirds of the rainforest's animals and plants.

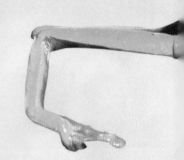

### Howler monkeys

Every morning in the Amazon rainforest, in South America, groups of howler monkeys howl and shriek. The noise is ear-splitting and can be heard up to five kilometres away. It warns other monkeys to stay away from their patch of forest.

◀ Howler monkeys are by far the loudest of all monkeys.

# Tree frogs

Tiny red-eyed tree frogs live in the canopy layer. They lay their eggs on leaves above rivers or ponds. When the tadpoles hatch, they drop straight down into the water and swim away.

▶ Sunbirds live in the rainforests of Africa and Asia.

## AWESOME!

Toucans use their famously long, brightly coloured beaks to reach fruit growing on branches that are too small to take their weight.

# Sunbird snacks

Sunbirds feed on sweet nectar from the rainforest flowers. They perch on a branch and use their long, downward-curving bills to reach deep inside a flower. They also eat insects and spiders.

▼ The southern tamandua – also known as the collared anteater – uses its claws for breaking open insect nests.

# Tamanduas

The southern tamandua climbs through the canopy at night, looking for ants and termites to eat. It licks up the insects with its long tongue. It has long claws for clinging on to branches, and can curl its tail around trees for extra grip.

11

# The understorey

Small trees, such as spindly palms and saplings, grow in the understorey, below the canopy. Here it is hot, damp and gloomy, as much of the light is blocked by the layers of leaves and branches above.

▶ The branches and trunks of the trees here are covered in trailing vines and creepers. These are often used by animals as climbing ropes.

## Sneaky snakes

Some understorey snakes are long, green and slender – and look like vines dangling from the trees. The vine snake sits on a branch, waiting for a lizard or mouse to pass by, then it strikes. By the time its prey spots the snake, it is too late to escape.

◀ Vine snakes also have heads shaped like leaves, making them very hard to spot.

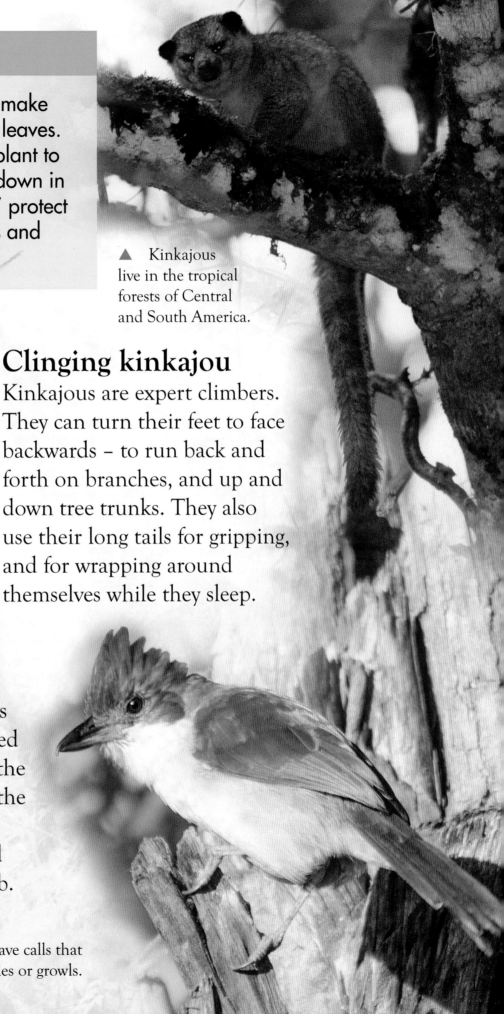

▲ Kinkajous live in the tropical forests of Central and South America.

## Clinging kinkajou

Kinkajous are expert climbers. They can turn their feet to face backwards – to run back and forth on branches, and up and down tree trunks. They also use their long tails for gripping, and for wrapping around themselves while they sleep.

▲ These tent-making bats are safe in the shelter they have made.

## Ant birds

Antshrikes are rainforest birds that build their nests in the understorey, but feed on insects and lizards on the forest floor. Some follow the armies of ants that march across the forest floor and eat the insects they disturb.

▶ Antshrikes have calls that sound like chuckles or growls.

▲ The bushmaster's colouring and patterns help it to catch its prey by surprise.

# Forest floor

Very little sunlight reaches the gloomy forest floor. A thick layer of roots, twigs and rotting leaves covers the ground. This is where a huge number of animals live and feed.

## Masters of disguise

Bushmasters are large, poisonous snakes from Central and South America. They can grow up to three metres long and have markings that blend with the forest floor, making them difficult to spot. When they are lying still, they look exactly like a harmless pile of leaves.

▼ Rotting leaves and plants put goodness back into the soil.

### AWESOME!

The royal antelopes of West Africa are shy, secretive and hard to spot. They are roughly the same size as rabbits, with legs as thin as pencils.

# Hissing cockroach

This creepy cockroach lives on the island of Madagascar, off Africa, where it shelters under logs and leaves on the forest floor. When it is disturbed, it makes a hissing sound by squeezing air out of tiny holes in its body.

▶ Its brown colour hides the cockroach among leaves and trees.

# Tapir trails

Tapirs eat fruit and leaves, which they search for in the morning and evening gloom. They follow well-worn paths through the forest to find the best fruit trees.

◀ The Malayan tapir's black-and-white coat helps to disguise it in patches of light and shade.

# Rainforest rivers

Flowing through the rainforest are large rivers and small streams. They are home to thousands of animals. Some swim in the water, while others come to feed and drink. Others live among plants and burrows along the banks.

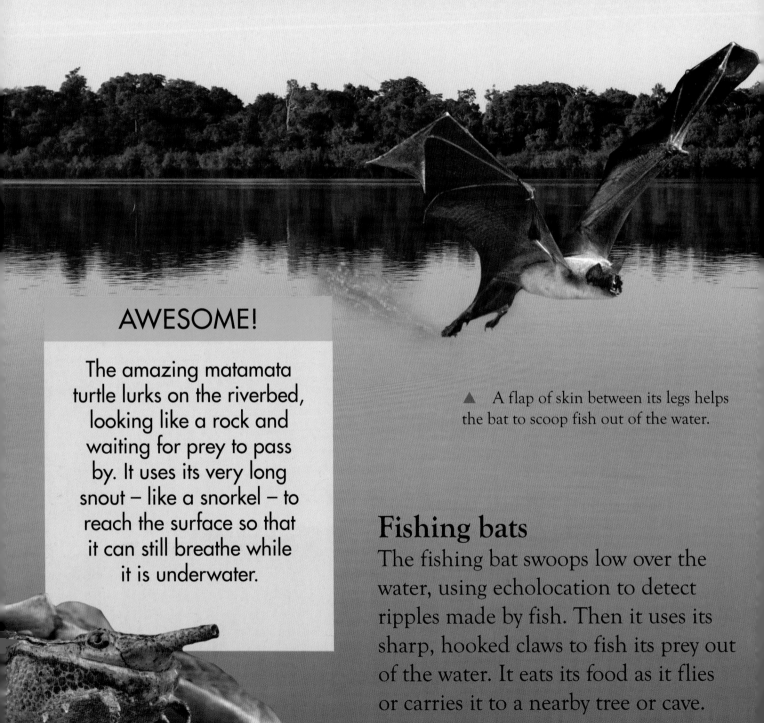

## AWESOME!

The amazing matamata turtle lurks on the riverbed, looking like a rock and waiting for prey to pass by. It uses its very long snout – like a snorkel – to reach the surface so that it can still breathe while it is underwater.

▲ A flap of skin between its legs helps the bat to scoop fish out of the water.

## Fishing bats

The fishing bat swoops low over the water, using echolocation to detect ripples made by fish. Then it uses its sharp, hooked claws to fish its prey out of the water. It eats its food as it flies or carries it to a nearby tree or cave.

# Water dragons

Water dragons are lizards that live by rivers in Australia and Southeast Asia. They spend most of their time resting on branches overhanging the water. If they sense danger, they quickly drop into the water many metres below.

▲ A water dragon resting on a branch above the water.

# Crafty catfish

A shovel-nosed catfish spends the day hiding under the water plants. At night, it comes out and starts to look for food on the riverbed. It uses its long, whiskery snout to poke around in the mud for worms and small fish.

▲ Rainforest rivers provide plenty of food, but they can also be very dangerous places – especially when they flood after heavy rains.

▶ Catfish are often caught by rainforest people for food.

# Amazon rainforest

The biggest rainforest on Earth grows along the banks of the Amazon River in South America. It covers an enormous six million square kilometres, which is almost the same size as Australia.

Ecuador

Amazon Rainforest

Brazil

South America

▼ Scarlet macaws.

▲ The Amazon rainforest makes up more than half of all the rainforest territory left in the world.

▼ The mighty Amazon River snakes through the world's largest rainforest.

## Chatty macaws

Macaws are large, brightly coloured parrots that live in the rainforest. They feed on nuts and seeds, cracking them open with their big, powerful beaks. Macaws often gather in flocks, calling, squawking and screaming to keep in touch with each other.

# Sleepy sloth

Sloths spend most of their lives hanging upside-down from trees. This helps them to save energy. Their long, curved claws lock tightly around a branch so that they don't fall off, even when they are asleep.

▶ Sloths spend most of their lives asleep!

## AWESOME!

One in ten of all known species of animals and plants lives in the Amazon rainforest. Incredibly, it is home to at least 2.5 million species of insects and 2,000 species of mammals and birds.

▶ One minute, the butterfly flashes bright blue...

▼ ...the next, it looks dull brown.

# Blue butterfly

On top, a blue morpho butterfly's wings are bright blue and black. Underneath, they are brown with dark spots. As the butterfly flies through the forest, its wings flash blue, then brown – so that it appears, then disappears. This makes it difficult for birds and other predators to catch it.

# Mammals

A huge range of mammals live in the rainforest, from tiny mice and rats to giant bats, apes and even elephants and rhinoceroses. They have all adapted to life in the trees and on the ground.

▲ Mammals such as these chorongo monkeys, from Ecuador in South America, have many different ways of finding food – while also staying safe.

## Pine-cone pangolins

Pangolins spend the day in burrows, then come out at night to feed on termites. When danger threatens, the pangolin rolls itself into a hard, tight ball to protect its soft belly from attack.

◀ The pangolin's body is covered in sharp-edged scales that overlap like the tiles on a roof.

## Sticky fingers

Aye ayes are odd-looking creatures from Madagascar, with a bushy tail, bat-like ears and huge, bright, orange eyes. They also have long, twig-like middle fingers for poking about under the bark of trees to search for juicy grubs.

◄ The aye aye finds grubs by listening out for their movements.

## Record rodents

The world's biggest rodents, capybaras look like giant guinea pigs. They live in large groups by rivers, where they feed on grass and water plants. They also eat their own droppings, which helps them to digest their food. With webbed feet for swimming, they are well adapted for life in the water.

▼ Capybaras are just as much at home in the water as they are on dry land.

# Forest hunters

Many of the top predators in the rainforests are mammals, such as big cats. They hunt and kill other animals. To do this, they need sharp senses and killer features – such as sharp teeth and claws.

## Jungle jaguar

Jaguars patrol the South American rainforests, looking for deer, tapirs and wild pigs. Sometimes, they drop down onto their prey from trees. They are also excellent swimmers, catching caimans and capybaras.

### AWESOME!

Sun bears live in Southeast Asian rainforests. They use their long, sharp claws and teeth to break open termite mounds to reach the insects inside. They also rip open tree trunks to reach wild bees.

▼ Jaguars have strong jaws and sharp teeth. They can kill their prey with a single bite.

## Clouded leopard

Clouded leopards live in the rainforests of Southeast Asia, and are brilliant climbers. They can hang upside down from the branches and climb down tree trunks head first. These leopards also drag their food up into trees to eat it.

▶ At night, clouded leopards come down from the trees to hunt for deer, pigs and monkeys.

## Tiger stripes

A tiger's stripy coat hides it in the undergrowth as it hunts deer, cattle and goats. It stalks its prey silently until it is within range. Then, it pounces. It brings its victim down with its huge front paws, then kills it with a lethal bite.

▼ ▲ Many big cats have markings that make them difficult to see. This means they can sneak up and pounce on their prey without being seen.

▶ Bengal tigers are found in India, China, Bangladesh, Indonesia and other Southeast Asian countries.

# On the move

Rainforest mammals have many ways of moving about to find food and to escape from enemies. Some swing or climb through the trees. Some can fly or glide from branch to branch. Others are excellent swimmers.

◀ Gibbons live in small family groups in the treetops. They use long, loud calls to defend their territory from other gibbons.

## Swinging gibbons

Gibbons are very fast, acrobatic apes. They swing from one branch to another, using their very long arms and strong, hook-shaped hands to hold on. Gibbons spend most of their lives in trees, and hardly ever go down to the ground.

## Flying foxes

Flying foxes, or fruit bats, feed on fruit and flower nectar, which they find by smell. They fly through the forest and use their sharp, curved claws to grip on to trees. During the day, they rest in the treetops, dangling upside down.

## AWESOME!

Tree kangaroos can hop across the ground but they spend most of their lives up in the trees. They have strong legs and feet for leaping and jumping, and sharp claws for climbing and gripping.

▲ Flying foxes have huge, leathery wings that can measure more than 1.5 metres across.

▼ River otters normally measure up to about 1.5 metres long – but giant otters can reach 1.8 metres.

## Giant otters

Giant otters look clumsy on land but are strong, graceful swimmers. They use their large, webbed feet as paddles and their long tails to steer as they drift around in the water. These otters normally hunt for fish, but they also eat small caimans and snakes.

# Tropical birds

Rainforest trees make perfect places for birds to find food, build nests and raise their young. Birds also live on the forest floor, where they forage for insects and worms among the roots and leaves.

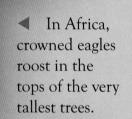

◀ In Africa, crowned eagles roost in the tops of the very tallest trees.

▲ Hoatzins are the size of chickens. They live in South America, in swampy areas around the Amazon and Orinoco rivers.

## Eagle-eyed hunters

Crown eagles have powerful legs and long, sharp talons for killing monkeys, small antelopes and mongooses. One of its favourite ways of hunting is to sit in a tree overlooking a waterhole, and then simply drop down onto its prey.

## Pitta patter

Pittas are brightly coloured birds that spend most of their time on the forest floor. They use their keen eyesight and sense of smell to find worms and snails to eat. Some smash the snail shells open on rocks and tree roots.

▲ Most pittas are found in Southeast Asia, but some species live in Australia and Africa.

## AWESOME!

The beautiful hyacinth macaw is the world's largest parrot, measuring about a metre from its head to the tip of its tail. It has blue feathers, a black beak and patches of bright yellow skin on its face.

◄ The cassowary may use its helmet as a battering ram for crashing through the forest undergrowth.

## Headstrong cassowary

Cassowaries are large, flightless birds that live in Australia and New Guinea. They stand around two metres tall. On their heads, they have odd, bony helmets. No one is quite sure why.

# Fruits and flowers

Many rainforest birds feed on leaves, fruits, buds, nuts, nectar and pollen. Some of these birds have special features, such as an extra-strong or extra-long beak, to help them to tackle their favourite food.

## Helpful hornbills

Rainforest plants need to spread out their seeds, and rely on birds and other animals to help them do this. Hornbills eat fruits and berries. As they fly, they pass droppings that contain lots of seeds from the food they've eaten.

▶ A macaw's beak is so strong that it can crack open rock-hard Brazil nuts.

◀ Hornbills use their large beaks to catch food, build nests, clean their feathers – and fight.

## Hover birds

Hummingbirds hover in front of flowers to feed on their sugary nectar. As the birds feed, they get covered in pollen, which they then carry to other flowers, allowing new seeds to grow.

▲ The hummingbird's long, thin beak is specially adapted to get deep into the flower.

## Nut crackers

Macaws eat all sorts of nuts and seeds, which they break open with their sharp, curved beaks. They also nibble at riverbank clay to get the essential salts and minerals that their body needs.

### AWESOME!

Hanging parrots from Asia hang upside down from branches. From a distance, they look like bunches of leaves – so their enemies leave them alone.

29

# Finding a mate

Male birds look for a female mate that can lay eggs that will hatch into young. Some make dance-like movements or show off their fabulous feathers, hoping that a female will pick them out. Others build shelters or use loud voices to call to females.

## Say it with sticks

Male satin bowerbirds build amazing stick shelters, called bowers, on the forest floor. They decorate them with shiny blue berries, fruits and flowers to attract a female. The females visit different bowers and choose the male with the best one.

▼ This male bowerbird has also collected artificial blue objects as gifts to attract a mate.

▼ Most birds of paradise come from New Guinea.

## AWESOME!

A male bellbird has a very loud voice for calling to females. It can be heard more than 0.8 kilometres away and sounds like a large, clanging bell.

# Birds of paradise

Birds of paradise live up to their name. The females are dull in colour – but the males have a spectacular plumage. The Count Raggi's bird of paradise fans and shakes its feathers to show off to females, sometimes hanging upside down from a branch.

# Pheasant feathers

A male great argus pheasant of Southeast Asia has very long tail and wing feathers. Once it has cleared a space on the forest floor, the male bird fans out its wings and 'dances' to show off its patterns.

▲ The pheasant's wing feathers are decorated with rows of large markings that look like eyes.

▶ The great argus pheasant can grow to two metres in length.

31

# Asian rainforests

In Asia, there are patches of rainforest in India and the countries of the southeast. Some of these tropical forests grow on the mainland, and some grow on scattered islands such as Borneo.

## Nosey monkeys

Male proboscis monkeys from Borneo are famous for their big, bulging noses. Amazingly, these outsized noses help the monkeys to attract mates. A male uses his nose like a loudspeaker to boost the sound of his call – and impress a female.

▲ Many amazing and unusual animals live in the rainforests of India and Southeast Asia.

▼ The nose of a male proboscis monkey can grow to more than ten centimetres long.

## Night vision

Tarsiers are very small creatures, with enormous eyes for spotting their prey of insects at night. They also have very long back legs and toes for climbing, clinging and leaping through trees.

▲ Each eye is the same size and weight as the tarsier's brain.

## Cat-like killers

Green cat snakes live among the trees overhanging the water, where their colouring makes them hard to see. At night, they hunt lizards and frogs. They inject their prey with poison, then swallow it whole.

▶ Green cat snakes have large, cat-like eyes – adapted for seeing well at night.

33

# Reptiles

Rainforest reptiles range from tiny, dwarf chameleons to enormous crocodiles and alligators. They can climb, swim and slither, and are found all over the forest, from the tall trees of the canopy to rivers and streams.

▼ Crocodiles have their eyes and nostrils on top of their heads, so that they can still see and breathe while in the water.

▼ Chameleons usually have green or brown markings to blend in with the rainforest trees.

## Chameleon colours

Chameleons are extraordinary creatures that can change colour, often to communicate and show what sort of mood they are in. If an intruder enters its territory, a chameleon will turn much darker in colour – to show an increase in fear and aggression.

# Crunching caiman

Caimans are related to alligators and crocodiles. The biggest is the black caiman, which can grow up to 4.5 metres long. It lurks in the water, waiting for prey to pass by, then it snaps them up with its sharp, pointed teeth.

▲ Black caimans live in slow-moving rivers and streams in South America.

# Walking on water

The basilisk lizard from Central America has an unusual way of escaping from its enemies. It jumps into the river and races across the surface, without falling in. When the danger is over, the lizard swims for the shore.

▲ To stop it from sinking, the lizard slaps at the water with its long legs, big feet and long, wide toes.

## AWESOME!

A chameleon can swivel each of its bulging, cone-shaped eyes separately. This is so it can look all around its body. When it sees prey, it focuses both eyes in the same direction.

# Snakes of the rainforest

Rainforests make brilliant homes for slithering snakes of all kinds. Snakes need warmth to stay active, but they also need shady places to avoid too much sunshine. There is also plenty of prey to feed on in rainforests – rodents, frogs, birds and insects.

▼ The eyelash viper is venomous, and can strike at its prey with lightning speed.

## Ssssupersized

Anacondas are enormous, reaching eight metres in length and weighing more than 225 kilograms. They can eat animals as large as deer, by wrapping their bodies around them and squeezing them to death.

## Eyelash vipers

The beautiful but deadly eyelash viper gets its name from the bristly scales above its eyes. These scales may have adapted in this way to break up the shape of the snake's body as it hides among the leaves.

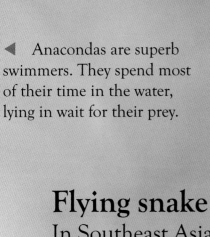

◄ Anacondas are superb swimmers. They spend most of their time in the water, lying in wait for their prey.

## Flying snake

In Southeast Asia, some snakes can glide through the air. First, they slither to the end of a branch and dangle in a J-shape. Then they take off. They can 'fly' up to 50 metres from one tree to another.

▼ Flying snakes don't have wings. They flatten out their bodies to catch the air.

## AWESOME!

The gaboon viper from Africa has the longest fangs of any snake. They are an awesome five centimetres long – that's about as long as your little finger.

# Insects

There are more types of insects in the rainforest than any other kind of animal. There are at least one million species – and there may be millions more, waiting to be discovered. They include tiny ants, giant beetles, huge butterflies and cleverly camouflaged stick insects.

## Cutting edge

Leaf-cutter ants are tiny but they are also incredibly strong. Each ant can carry a piece of leaf weighing around 50 times its own weight. They collect the leaves to make gardens, in their nests, where they grow a special fungus. The fungus is their food.

## AWESOME!

Paper wasps are master builders. They create umbrella-shaped nests high up in the trees. They make the 'paper' for their nests from dead wood and plant stems, which they chew up and mix with their spit.

◀ Leaf-cutter ants snip the leaves with their sharp jaws, and then carry the pieces back to their nests.

## Jungle giraffe

This little weevil from Madagascar is one of the oddest-looking insects in the rainforest. The male is about 2.5 centimetres long, with a giraffe-like head and neck about half as long as the rest of its body. No one is exactly sure what this extra-long neck is for.

▶ A male weevil could possibly use its neck to fight with rivals to win a female mate.

▼ This Richmond birdwing butterfly, of Australia, is large – but it is only about half the size of the Queen Alexandra birdwing.

## Record-breaker

Birdwing butterflies are very large. The Queen Alexandra birdwing lives in a small patch of rainforest in Papua New Guinea. With a wingspan of 28 centimetres, it is the biggest butterfly in the world. Red hairs on its body warn hungry enemies that it is poisonous.

# Masters of disguise

Many rainforest insects use colours and patterns to hide from hungry predators. Some also disguise themselves to catch their prey by surprise, while others pretend to be more dangerous than they really are.

## Double trouble

A false leaf katydid looks just like a dead, brown leaf on the forest floor. If this disguise does not work, it has another trick. Quick as a flash, it can flick its wings open to show off its eyespots. This startles a predator long enough for the insect to escape.

▶ Over time, the colours of this mantis have adapted to look like those of an orchid's flowers.

◀ This katydid's wings look just like leaves, right down to the tiny veins.

## Perfect petals

The orchid mantis has the perfect disguise. Its body is the same colour as the orchid flower it rests on – even its legs and wings look like petals. The mantis stays still, waiting for small insects to pass by.

▼ The mantis grabs insects with its front legs, then gobbles them up.

## AWESOME!

Some rainforest moths – such as this comet moth from Madagascar – have large, eye-like markings on their wings. These may frighten enemies away, or trick them into leaving the moth's real head alone.

▼ Just like real sticks, stick insects are sometimes covered in lichen or moss.

## Giant, walking stick

Some rainforest stick insects can grow as long as your arm – but they are extremely difficult to spot. Many have a long, thin, brown body and look exactly like a stick. Some also pretend to be dead if they are attacked.

# Food and feeding

Insects make tasty snacks for lots of rainforest animals. But the forest also supplies insects with plenty of food to eat. Some insects feed on leaves and flowers. Others eat each other!

▲ Driver ants travel in enormous swarms, many millions strong.

## Praying mantis

The praying mantis is a fearsome predator. It snatches moths, crickets, grasshoppers and flies by shooting out its long front legs. These mantises also feed on each other – females sometimes even eat their mates!

▼ The mantis's legs have sharp spikes on them for pinning down their prey.

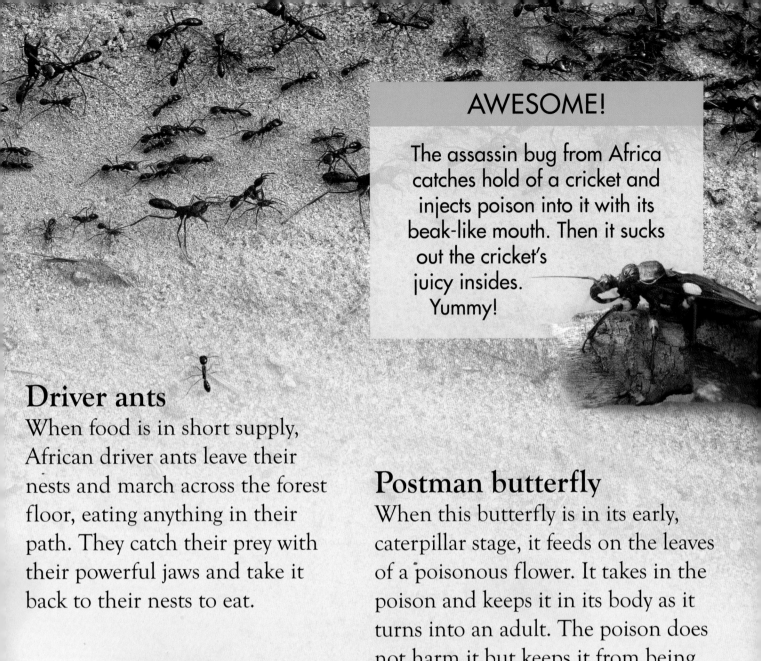

The assassin bug from Africa catches hold of a cricket and injects poison into it with its beak-like mouth. Then it sucks out the cricket's juicy insides. Yummy!

## Driver ants

When food is in short supply, African driver ants leave their nests and march across the forest floor, eating anything in their path. They catch their prey with their powerful jaws and take it back to their nests to eat.

## Postman butterfly

When this butterfly is in its early, caterpillar stage, it feeds on the leaves of a poisonous flower. It takes in the poison and keeps it in its body as it turns into an adult. The poison does not harm it but keeps it from being eaten by predators.

▶ This insect was named the postman butterfly because it follows the same path from flower to flower every day.

43

# African rainforests

Rainforests grow in West and Central Africa, mostly along the banks of the River Congo. The Congo rainforest is the second largest in the world, after the mighty Amazon of South America.

▲ There are also small patches of rainforest on the island of Madagascar, off the east coast of Africa.

◄ Okapis have big ears and a dark, velvety coat with stripes on their bottom and legs.

## The shy okapi

The okapi is a timid and secretive animal, related to the giraffe. It browses on rainforest trees and shrubs, pulling off the leaves with its long tongue.

▶ Chimpanzees live in large family groups in the rainforests of Central and West Africa.

## Sleepy chimps

Chimpanzees feed on fruit, leaves and insects, but also work together to hunt larger animals such as colobus monkeys. At night, the adults build leafy nests in the treetops where they and their young can sleep, safe from night-time predators.

## AWESOME!

The giant African millipede has around 256 legs and grows up to 38 centimetres long – that's about the length from your elbow to your fingertips. When it is threatened, it curls up into a tight ball on the forest floor.

## Elephant shrews

Elephant shrews, or sengis, are not actually shrews – they are related to elephants. They have a long, bendy snout that can twist and turn in search of food, just like an elephant's trunk does.

▶ Sengis are small and furry, with a scaly tail and long legs, which they use for hopping about.

# Amphibians

Amphibians live all over the rainforest. They range from frogs and toads to salamanders and caecilians. Some live high in the canopy to avoid hungry predators. Others are superbly disguised on the forest floor.

▼ The marine toad, or cane toad, can weigh a whopping two kilograms!

## Greedy guts

The marine toad is found along the banks of the River Amazon. It eats anything it can fit into its mouth, including large insects, small snakes, lizards and mice. It will even eat bees straight out of their hive – and its own young, if it is very hungry.

## AWESOME!

Tomato frogs from Madagascar have sneaky ways of protecting themselves. They puff up their body, then ooze out a sticky glue from their skin, which gums up an attacker's eyes and mouth.

# Rubbery eels

Rubber eels are from a group of amphibians called caecilians. They spend a lot of their time burrowing underground, but they are also good swimmers. Caecilians are nearly blind and find their food – of insects and earthworms – mostly by taste and smell.

▶ Leaf-like skin texture.

## Frogs in disguise

With its blotchy brown markings, the long-nosed horned frog of Southeast Asia looks just like a dry, dead leaf. Its skin has folds that look like leaf veins, and it has spiky horns on its head that break up its frog shape. Tree frogs, such as the one below, are also very well camouflaged.

▲ Until this frog moves, it is almost impossible to see against the forest floor!

▼ This beautiful peacock tree frog is from Tanzania, in Africa.

# Fabulous frogs

The most common amphibians living in the rainforest are frogs. There are many different kinds – some tiny, some huge, some brightly coloured, some well hidden. Others are poisonous, while some appear to fly.

## Beware: poison!

The poison dart frog's brightly coloured skin is a message to its enemies. It warns others that this tiny frog is dangerous to eat. Its skin contains a poison so strong that a single drop can kill a monkey in just a few seconds.

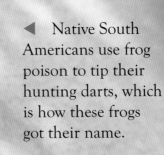

◄ Native South Americans use frog poison to tip their hunting darts, which is how these frogs got their name.

# Flying frogs

In the rainforests of Southeast Asia, there are frogs that can glide from branch to branch. To escape from predators, they stretch out the webs of skin between their long fingers and toes, then launch themselves from a tree, like little parachutes.

▲ Asian flying frogs can glide over a distance of about 15 metres at a time.

◄ By night, most tree frogs hunt for insects. By day, they hide in cracks and holes.

## Tree frogs

Tree frogs are brilliant climbers. They have round, sticky pads on their fingers and toes to help them cling to leaves and tree bark. The skin on their bellies, which is loose and sticky, also helps them to grip the trees.

## AWESOME!

The gigantic goliath frog from Africa is the biggest frog in the world. It can grow to more than 30 centimetres in length. It lives near rivers, where it feeds mostly on water plants.

# Fish

The rivers and streams that run through the rainforests are home to a wide variety of fish. In the Amazon River alone, there are around 5,000 different fish species. Often, even small pools and puddles are full of life.

## Peckish piranhas

Armed with rows of razor-sharp teeth, piranhas swim and hunt in large groups. By hunting together, they can tackle animals much larger than themselves, such as caimans, manatees and anacondas. Some piranhas are vegetarians, feeding on fruit and seeds.

▲ Piranhas have such sharp teeth that local people sometimes use them as scissors or knives.

# Piracucu

The piracucu, or arapaima, is a huge fish that lives in the River Amazon. It can reach two metres in length and weigh up to 200 kilograms. It feeds on fish, shellfish and even small land animals.

▲ The piracucu is a torpedo-shaped fish with dark green scales and red markings.

# Rainforest fishing

The fire-mouth panchax gets its name from the male's red throat. These fish live in small pools of water that fill up in the wet season. They feed on insects and grow quickly, laying lots of eggs. When the dry season comes, the pools dry up and the fish die, but their eggs are left behind in the mud and hatch as soon as it rains again.

## AWESOME!

Electric eels feed mainly on other fish. They give off strong electric shocks to stun their prey and warn off predators.

▶ Local rainforest people hunt fish, such as the piracucu, for their meat. Traditionally, they catch the fish with nets and spears, or with bows and arrows.

# Rainforest spiders

Thousands of different kinds of spiders live in the rainforests. Some are tiny; others are as big as plates. Some spin huge webs to catch their prey; others hunt for food on the forest floor.

## Super spider

The goliath bird-eating spider from South America is the biggest spider in the world (by weight). It lives on the forest floor and comes out at night to hunt. It lies in wait, then pounces and bites into its victim with its poisonous fangs.

## Spinning tales

Orb weaver spiders spin webs as big as bed sheets between the rainforest trees. Then the female sits in front of the web, waiting for prey. The webs are big enough to catch animals as large as frogs and hummingbirds.

◄ Including its long, hairy legs, the goliath spider can grow as large as a dinner plate.

▶ This jumping spider is sitting near a flower, waiting to pounce.

◀ Orb weaver webs are so strong that rainforest people can use them to make fishing nets.

## Sneaky spiders

Jumping spiders feed on smaller spiders. They will sit on a spider's web, looking like a trapped insect. They might even pluck on the web to make it vibrate, as if they are stuck and struggling. When the web's owner comes to investigate, the jumping spider pounces.

### AWESOME!

The Brazilian wandering spider is one of the world's most poisonous spiders. When it is threatened, it lifts up its front legs and shows off its deadly fangs.

# More creepy crawlies

Spiders are not the only creepy crawlies at home in the rainforests. There are hundreds of other animals – including scorpions, millipedes, centipedes, leeches and snails – hiding among the trees and on the forest floor.

## AWESOME!

Apple snails live in rivers but lay their eggs on the trunks of trees. This keeps them safe from hungry fish. When the baby snails hatch out, they drop straight into the water below.

## Bloodsuckers

Leeches feed on the blood of other animals. They sink their sharp teeth into a victim, then hang on tight. When full, they drop off. A leech can suck up 15 times its own weight in blood in just one meal.

◀ Once a leech has filled up with blood, it does not need to eat for another six months or so.

## Giant in a small world

The Amazonian giant centipede is big and fierce enough to hunt animals such as insects, large spiders, lizards, frogs and snakes. It uses a pair of sharp claws to tear into its prey and inject it with poison.

◀ This giant centipede's bright colours warn its enemies that it is poisonous.

## Sting in the tail

The gigantic emperor scorpion has a glossy, black body, large pinchers and a long, curled tail with a deadly sting at the end. The scorpion uses its sting in self-defence and for catching insect prey. It hunts at night, using hairs on its body to sense the whereabouts of its prey.

▲ Adult scorpions can grow up to 20 centimetres long and can weigh 30 grams.

# Australasian rainforests

In Australia, there are three small patches of rainforest along the northeastern coast. They are all that is left of a much bigger, ancient forest. To the north lies the island of New Guinea, which still has large areas of rainforest.

▶ The Blyth's hornbill is famous for its big, bony beak. It lives in the rainforests of Papua New Guinea.

◀ Some of the rainforest in New Guinea has yet to be explored by people.

## Duck-billed burrower

Duck-billed platypuses live in rivers and streams, where they use their duck-like bills to scoop up worms, insects and shellfish from the riverbed. They dig burrows, with underwater entrances, along the riverbank.

◀ Platypuses store food in their cheeks, then rise to the surface to chew and swallow it.

## Security conscious

For safety, the female Blyth's hornbill builds her nest inside a hollow tree trunk, then seals herself in behind a wall of mud. There is a small slit for the male to pass through food. She stays there for several weeks, until her chicks are ready to leave the nest.

▶ Ghost bats are named after their very thin, ghostly-looking wings.

## Flying phantoms

Deathly pale ghost bats fly silently through the Australian rainforest at night. They find their prey – of mice, lizards and insects – using echolocation. Then they pin it down with their sharp claws and kill it with a bite to the neck.

## AWESOME!

Over the last 20 years, more than a thousand new kinds of animals and plants have been found in the rainforests of New Guinea.

# Animals in danger

Every day, huge areas of rainforest are destroyed. Trees are cut down for their timber or burned to make space for farms, mines and new roads. This has a devastating effect on animals, which are left with nowhere to live or find food. Many of them are in danger of becoming extinct.

## Rare rhinos

Sumatran rhinos are the smallest type of rhino. They once roamed across large parts of Asia, but today only a few hundred survive. Their close relative, the Javan rhino, may already be extinct.

▼ Sumatran rhinos now live in small patches of forest on the islands of Sumatra and Borneo.

## NOT SO AWESOME!

No one has seen a Spix's macaw in the wild for more than 13 years. There are, however, about 100 of these macaws living in zoos and wildlife parks.

◀ The Amazon manatee lives in the Amazon River, where it feeds on water plants.

## Disappearing manatees

Large herds of Amazon manatees were once found, but so many have been killed for their meat and fat that they are now very rare. The destruction of the forest around them means they also have a lot less food to eat.

▶ Lowland gorillas feed mostly on fruit – around 100 different kinds have been found in their diet.

## Lowland losses

Lowland gorillas live in the rainforests of Central Africa. Huge parts of these forests have been cut down for timber. The gorillas are also hunted for their meat, and for body parts used in traditional medicine.

▶ On the islands of Borneo and Sumatra, in Southeast Asia, orangutans are under serious threat.

# Saving the animals

Around the world, people are working hard to save the rainforests and their wildlife. Some patches of forest are being set aside as parks, and new forests are being planted. Conservationists are also teaching people and businesses how to use the forests without damaging them.

## Success story

In the 1980s, only 200 golden lion tamarins were left. Luckily, government and conservation groups took action to protect their habitat. Also, 140 zoos around the world began to breed tamarins in captivity, returning them to the wild when they are ready.

◀ Golden lion tamarins come from the rainforests of Brazil in South America.

## Threatening fungus

Many kinds of rainforest frogs are being wiped out by a deadly fungus. Biologists in places such as Panama are trying to save them. They collect the frogs and transport them to special containers, in zoos, where they can keep them alive and safe.

▶ This lemur tree frog lives in Costa Rica, Panama and Colombia.

## Rescuing orangutans

Some organisations adopt homeless orangutans and look after them until they can be released back into the wild, in specially protected patches of forest. Others try to stop orangutans being caught and sold as pets.

## NOT SO AWESOME!

Today, there are only about 40,000 orangutans left in Borneo, and around 7,500 in Sumatra. If we don't protect them, there may be none left in 10 years' time.

# Glossary

**Adapted** Gradually developed to suit a particular purpose or environment.

**Amphibians** Animals, such as frogs and toads, that have smooth, damp skin. Amphibians lay their eggs in the water.

**Bill** Another name for an animal's beak, especially when it is long or flattened.

**Birds** Animals, such as toucans and macaws, that have wings, feathers and beaks.

**Burrow** A hole, dug in the ground, where animals live or raise their young.

**Caecilian** An amphibian that looks more like a snake or earthworm. Caecilians live mainly hidden in the ground.

**Camouflage** Body patterns, colours and shapes that help to hide animals among the natural features of their habitat.

**Canopy** A thick, green roof of treetops that stretches over the rainforest, beneath the emergent trees.

**Captivity** When animals are kept in wildlife parks or zoos – sometimes for their protection.

**Conservation** Protecting or looking after an animal, plant or place for the future.

**Echolocation** How some animals use sound to find food or their way around. They send out sounds and detect the returning echoes.

**Emergents** A rainforest's tallest trees, which stick out above the canopy level.

**Equator** The invisible 'central line' that runs around the middle of the Earth.

**Extinct** A species of plant or animal that has died out for ever.

**Fangs** Long, hollow teeth that snakes and some other animals use to inject poison into their prey.

**Fish** Animals, such as catfish and piranhas, that have fins and sleek, streamlined bodies. Many species of fish have scaly bodies.

**Gliding** When an animal flies without flapping wings or other body parts.

**Habitat** The place where a species of animal or plant is found and is adapted to living in.

**Insects** Animals, such as butterflies and ants, that have six legs and three parts to their bodies.

**Mammals** Animals, such as jaguars and orangutans, that have hair or fur covering their bodies. Mammals feed their young on milk produced by the mother.

**Nectar** A sugar-rich liquid made by plants and used as food by birds and insects.

**Orchid** A plant that grows in the rainforest and has beautiful flowers.

**Plumage** Another word for a bird's feathers, especially if they are long or brightly coloured.

**Pollen** A fine powder, made by plants, that helps to produce seeds and new plants.

**Predator** An animal that hunts and feeds on other animals.

**Prey** An animal that is hunted and eaten by another animal.

**Reptiles** Animals, such as lizards and snakes, that have scaly skin. Reptiles lay eggs that have soft shells.

**Scales** Small, overlapping flaps that grow from the skin of fish and some other animals.

**Species** A group of living things that have similar features. Living things of the same species can mate and produce young.

**Tropical** Describes things that are found in the hottest parts of the world, around the equator. The regions to the north and south of the equator are known as the tropics.

**Understorey** The layer of rainforest plants and animals found beneath the canopy and above the forest floor.

**Venom** A poisonous substance that an animal uses to stun, harm or kill its enemies or prey.

# Index

# Further Information

## BOOKS

**Lifesize: Rainforest**
By Anita Ganeri (Kingfisher, 2014)

**First Animal Encyclopedia: Seas and Oceans**
By Anna Claybourne
(A & C Black, 2014)

**First Animal Encyclopedia**
By Anita Ganeri (A & C Black, 2013)

**Animals on the Edge: Gorilla**
By Anna Claybourne
(A & C Black, 2012)

**Bloomin' Rainforests**
(Horrible Geography series)
By Anita Ganeri (Scholastic, 2008)

## ONLINE RESOURCES

**BBC Nature**
See videos and pictures, and read information about rainforest life at:
http://www.bbc.co.uk/nature/habitats/Tropical_and_subtropical_moist_broadleaf_forests

**National Geographic**
Find out more about the rainforests and the dangers they face at:
http://environment.nationalgeographic.com/environment/habitats/rainforest-profile

**Rainforest Action Network**
Discover what is being done to protect the rainforests at:
http://ran.org